D1199216

HOW
SPIDER TRICKED
SNAKE

Copyright © 1989 American Teacher Publications

Published by Raintree Publishers

Library of Congress number: 89-3581

Library of Congress Cataloging in Publication Data.

Benitez, Mirna.
　　How spider tricked snake / Mirna Benitez; illustrated by Dorothea Sierra.
　　(Real readers)
　　Summary: An easy-to-read Jamaican folk tale featuring Anasi the spider.
　　1. Anansi (Legendary character). [1. Anansi (Legendary character) 2. Folklore—Jamaica.] I. Sierra, Dorothea, ill. I. Title. II. Series.
PZ8.1.B413Ho　1989　398.2′452544—dc19　[E]　　　　　　　　89-3581

ISBN 0-8172-3524-8

　2 3 4 5 6 7 8 9 0　　93 92 91 90 89

How Spider Tricked Snake

by Mirna Benitez
illustrated by Dorothea Sierra

Raintree Publishers
Milwaukee

One day Spider went to see Tiger. Tiger was the king of all the animals. As the king, Tiger had a say about everything that went on.

"O, King," said Spider. "I want everyone to think of me when it is time to tell a story. Please, I wish that all stories could be called Spider stories."

4

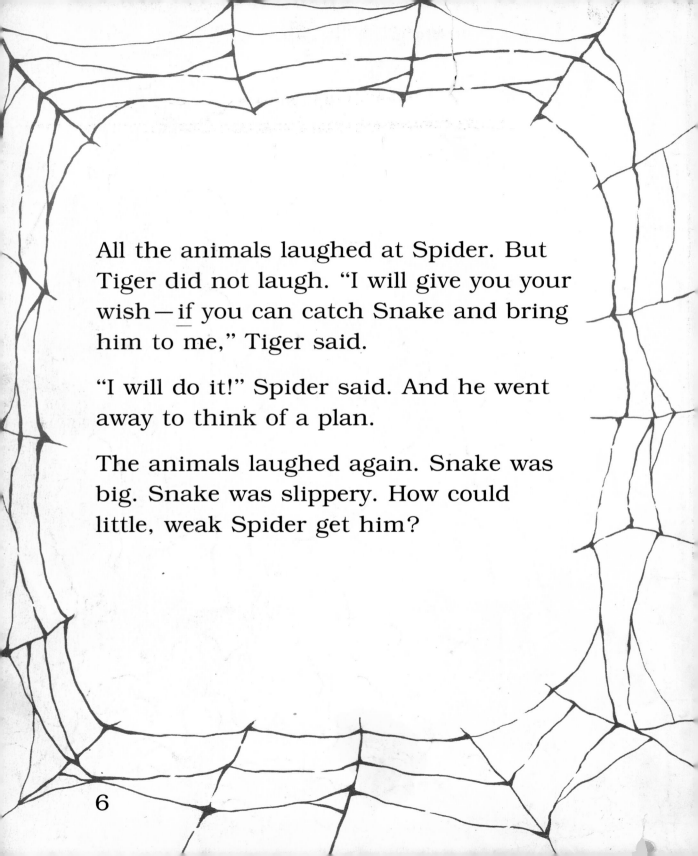

All the animals laughed at Spider. But Tiger did not laugh. "I will give you your wish—if you can catch Snake and bring him to me," Tiger said.

"I will do it!" Spider said. And he went away to think of a plan.

The animals laughed again. Snake was big. Snake was slippery. How could little, weak Spider get him?

Spider was little. Spider was weak. But he <u>was</u> a good thinker. He thought and thought. Then he jumped up. He had a plan!

"I will hide a vine in the grass," Spider said. "I will put berries next to the vine. Snake will come to eat the berries. Then WHAM! I will pull the vine all around Snake. That is how I will catch Snake!"

Spider did what he said he would do. Then he hid and waited for Snake.

Soon, along came Snake. He saw the berries. He saw the vine. He saw Spider, too.

"Ummmmmm," Snake said. He went to the berries. He ate them. Spider pulled the vine, but Snake was too slippery. He went under the vine. Then slip, slip, slip, away Snake went.

"My plan did not work," said Spider.

"I need a new plan," Spider said. He thought and thought. Then he jumped up. He had a plan!

"I will dig a big hole," Spider said. "I will put bananas in the hole. Then I will put grease on the sides of the hole. Snake will go in the hole to eat the bananas. Then SLOOSH! The sides of the hole will be too slippery. Snake will not get out. That is how I will catch Snake!"

Spider did what he said he would do. Then he hid and waited for Snake.

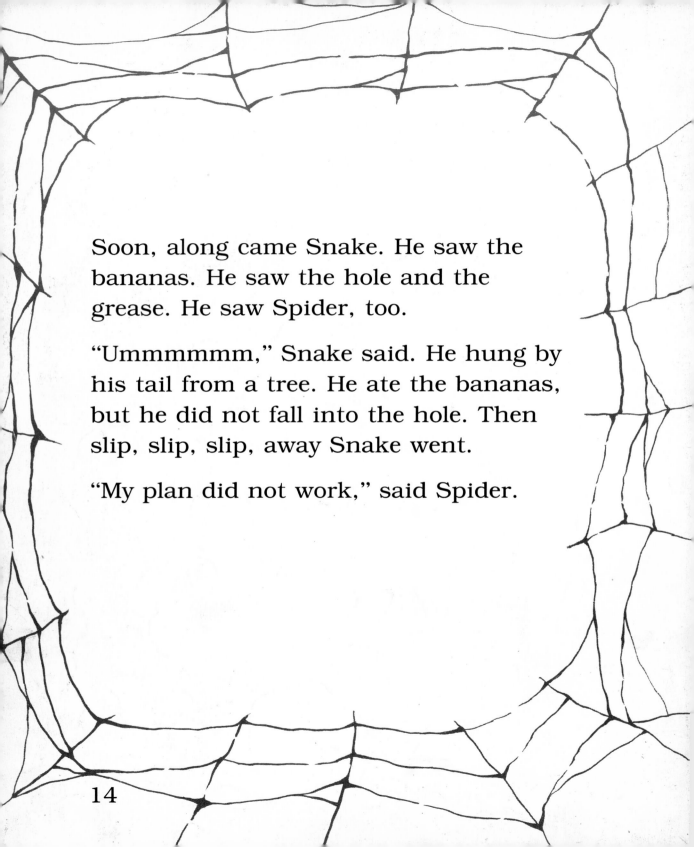

Soon, along came Snake. He saw the bananas. He saw the hole and the grease. He saw Spider, too.

"Ummmmmm," Snake said. He hung by his tail from a tree. He ate the bananas, but he did not fall into the hole. Then slip, slip, slip, away Snake went.

"My plan did not work," said Spider.

14

"I need a new plan," Spider said. He thought and thought. Then he jumped up. He had a plan!

"I will make a trap and hang it from a tree," Spider said. "I will put an egg in the trap. Snake will come to eat the egg. Then WHOOSH! The trap will close over Snake. That is how I will catch Snake!"

Spider did what he said he would do. Then he hid and waited for Snake.

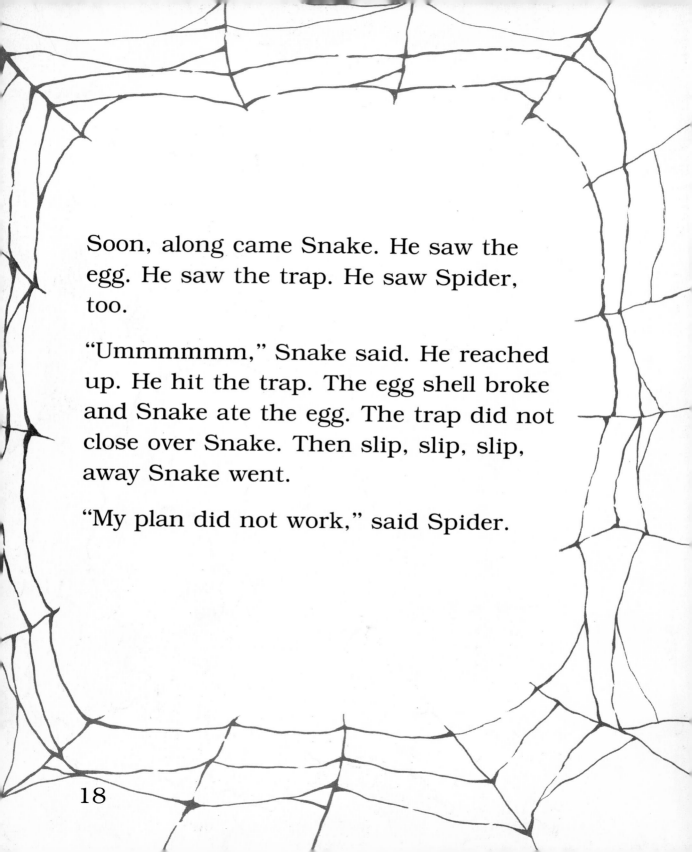

Soon, along came Snake. He saw the egg. He saw the trap. He saw Spider, too.

"Ummmmmm," Snake said. He reached up. He hit the trap. The egg shell broke and Snake ate the egg. The trap did not close over Snake. Then slip, slip, slip, away Snake went.

"My plan did not work," said Spider.

Spider sat down to think again. He
did not catch Snake with the vine. He
did not catch Snake with the hole. He
did not catch Snake with the trap.
Spider thought, "I did not catch Snake
when I hid and waited for him."

Then Spider jumped up. He had a plan.
"I think Snake knows I want to catch
him!" Spider said. "Maybe I can get
Snake to <u>let</u> me catch him!"

So, Spider went to see Snake. "I am
mad at you, Spider," said Snake. "You
are trying to catch me!"

"Yes, Snake. You are right," said Spider.
"I did want to catch you. I wanted to see
if you are longer than the big bamboo
tree."

"Is that all?" said Snake. "I am much
longer! Let's go to the bamboo tree. I
will show you."

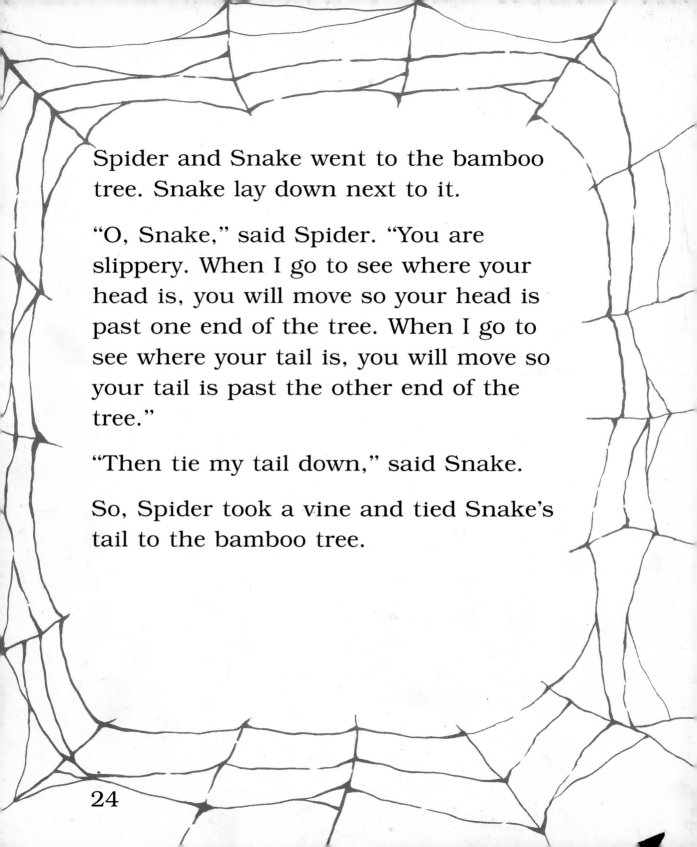

Spider and Snake went to the bamboo tree. Snake lay down next to it.

"O, Snake," said Spider. "You are slippery. When I go to see where your head is, you will move so your head is past one end of the tree. When I go to see where your tail is, you will move so your tail is past the other end of the tree."

"Then tie my tail down," said Snake.

So, Spider took a vine and tied Snake's tail to the bamboo tree.

"O, Snake," said Spider. "You are slippery. I will take a vine and tie you in the middle so you won't slip."

So, Spider took a vine and tied Snake's middle to the bamboo tree.

"See," said Snake. "I am much longer than the bamboo tree."

26

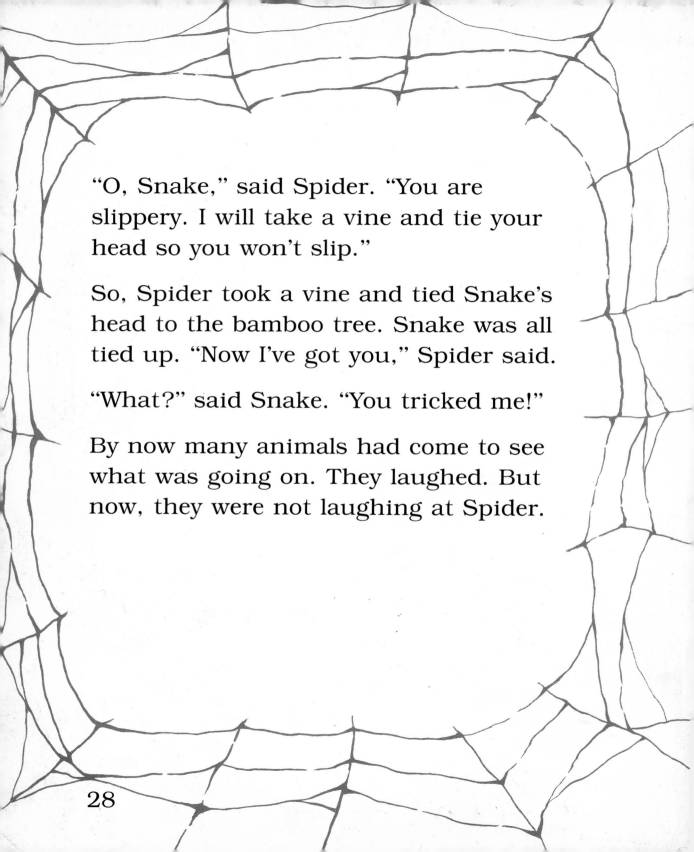

"O, Snake," said Spider. "You are slippery. I will take a vine and tie your head so you won't slip."

So, Spider took a vine and tied Snake's head to the bamboo tree. Snake was all tied up. "Now I've got you," Spider said.

"What?" said Snake. "You tricked me!"

By now many animals had come to see what was going on. They laughed. But now, they were not laughing at Spider.

All the animals helped bring Snake to Tiger. Tiger laughed when he saw Snake all tied up.

"Well, Spider," said Tiger. "You will get your wish. From this day on all stories will be called Spider stories. Now tell me, just how did you get Snake?"

Then Spider told the story of "How Spider Tricked Snake."

To this day, people still tell this story. And Spider still has his wish.

Sharing the Joy of Reading

Beginning readers enjoy reading books on their own. Reading a book is a worthwhile activity in and of itself for a young reader. However, a child's reading can be even more rewarding if it is shared. This sharing can enhance your child's appreciation — both of the book and of his or her own abilities.

Now that your child has read **How Spider Tricked Snake**, you can help extend your child's reading experience by encouraging him or her to:

- Retell the story or key concepts presented in this story in his or her own words. The retelling can be oral or written.

- Create a picture of a favorite character, event, or concept from this book.

- Express his or her own ideas and feelings about the characters in this book and other things the characters might do.

Here is a special activity that you and your child can do together to further extend the appreciation of this book: This book is an example of a folktale, a story that is wonderful for reading aloud. You and your child may have already read aloud other folktales such as *The Three Bears, The Gingerbread Boy,* or *Cinderella.* Pick a folktale you may have in a book at home, or select a folktale from the library to read aloud to your child. Your child can then read aloud to you using this book, **How Spider Tricked Snake**.